BATTLING THOR

BATTLING THOR

BY
EUGENE DALE SCHWARTZLOW

PALMETTO
PUBLISHING
Charleston, SC
www.PalmettoPublishing.com

Copyright © 2024 by Eugene Dale Schwartzlow

All rights reserved

No portion of this book may be reproduced, stored in a retrieval system, or transmitted in any form by any means–electronic, mechanical, photocopy, recording, or other–except for brief quotations in printed reviews, without prior permission of the author.

Hardcover ISBN: 979-8-8229-5313-0
Paperback ISBN: 979-8-8229-5314-7
eBook ISBN: 979-8-8229-5315-4

TABLE OF CONTENTS

Preface · vii

The Beginning · 1

American Search and Rescue Team called up · 14

The Turnover · 64

Returning Home · 75

Post-Operation Reflections · 76

Follow-up Actions · 87

Awards and Recognition · 91

About the Author · 93

PREFACE

In 1971, I was a Captain of the Marines. I was assigned to an accompanied tour of duty as the Executive Officer of Marine Barracks Iceland. One of my additional duties was to serve as the officer in charge of the American Air-Ground Search and Rescue (SAR) Team of Keflavík.

The SAR mission had been overlooked for several years. When I considered it, I found an outstanding inventory of ski and ice-climbing equipment as well as ropes and many other rescues items. I got quite excited about the possibility of having our Marines trained to do SAR. When I checked with the Marine Barracks Commanding Officer, Major Dick Weidner, he was all for it and thought it would do much to further our relationship with the Icelanders.

For the next two years, we conducted quarterly training exercises with the Icelandic *Flugbjörgunarsveitin*, which is their search and rescue. The training paved the way for us to be called upon when disaster struck in 1973.

In 1997, I retired from the Marine Corps as a colonel after completing thirty years, ten months, and nine days of active service. It wasn't until after I retired that I pulled together my notes, charts, maps, and old newspaper clippings and completed putting my thoughts together.

Battling Thor is my way of documenting the event and the accomplishments of our small group of Americans who were trying their best to help the Icelanders. I hope you find it interesting.

THE BEGINNING

22 January 1973

HEIMAEY, WESTMANN ISLANDS

In January 1973, it became clear to all who lived on Iceland's island of Heimaey why it is called "the Land of Frost and Fire."

Local inhabitants said that when three conditions were met, something terrible would happen on their island home. One was that the old town well would be closed. The second was that the town would grow beyond a certain boundary. The third was that the priest's son would become priest. Well, it happened. In 1971, a small child fell down the city well, and they decided to close it forever. In 1972, the town expanded and grew beyond the mythical boundary. And last, in 1973, one week before disaster struck, the priest's son became priest.

Here is what the island looked like before the disaster struck (See Figure 1).

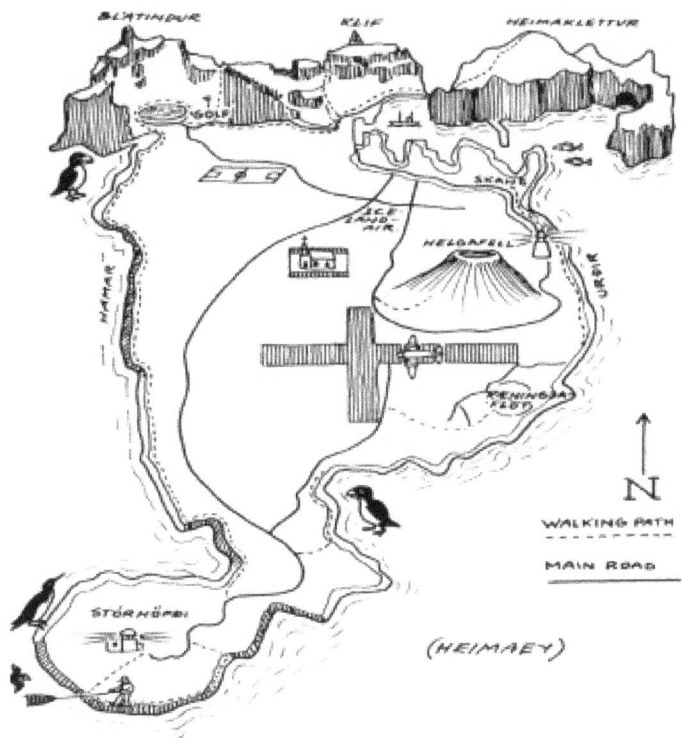

Figure 1. Drawing given to me of the way the island looked before the eruption.

EUGENE DALE SCHWARTZLOW

At 2200 on 22 January 1973, seismic tremors started to shake the Westmann Islands. They lasted until midnight. By 0200, the earth split open just about a kilometer outside the eastern limits of the town of Heimaey on the island bearing the same name. The fissure opened on the last remaining active farm on the island, *Kirkjubaer* (church farm). It was the land owned by the priest. Within two hours, the fissure had grown to nearly two kilometers long.

The wall of fire could be seen from as far away as the mainland of the island—eight miles away. It was throwing hot liquid and hot lava hundreds of feet into the air. Due to the five-thousand-year-old volcano, Helgafell, which was nearby, the initial lava flow was away from town to the sea. Below is a photo I extracted from a postcard that showed the situation on 23 January (See figure 2):

Figure 2. The eruption on 23 January

By evening, the fissure partially closed and a cone was formed on the northeast end.

BATTLING THOR

THE EVACUATION

At the time of the eruption, there were 5,247 residents and a few outsiders on the island. By 0300, all that were able, except firefighters, police, and a few government officials, were boarding seventy to seventy-five fishing boats that were tied up in the harbor. By 0600, nearly four thousand of the residents were ashore on the mainland at Thorlakshofn. Within two hours, most were transported to Reykjavík, the capital, where they were quickly dispersed to shelters and homes of relatives. By late afternoon, all were settled somewhere. Upon boarding the buses, all the people were registered, and the list was given to the police. Up to this point the island residents controlled the evacuation. Once reaching the mainland, the Icelandic Civil Defense and Red Cross was activated, and the responsibility was shifted to the Icelandic authorities. By the morning of the twenty-fifth, all students were registered in Reykjavík schools. Shown below is a newspaper photo of the people being relocated to Reykjavík on the twenty-fourth (See figure 3).

Figure 3 Newspaper coverage on 24 January

The remaining evacuation was by air and fishing boats making a second run. Flugfélag Íslands Airlines soon had three Fokker Friendship Aircraft evacuating people. By late afternoon on the twenty-third, all but one or two hundred had been evacuated and fifty police had been flown in from Reykjavík. Later, the NATO base was asked to provide two large Jolly Green Giants and a Hercu-

3

les helicopter to evacuate the elderly and hospitalized patients that were on the island. They moved sixty-seven people.

DAY 2: 24 JANUARY

On the second day, it was clear the volcano was growing in ferocity. By 1100, there were three craters erupting on the northeast end of the fissure. They were very close to the town. Lava was flowing from all three. Fortunately, most of the flowage was northeast toward the sea. Unfortunately, the sideward motion of the flowage went toward town. By 1100, the first cluster of houses was in the lava flow.

Eruption material such as pumice and scoria were growing rapidly. In several places, it was several feet thick. By 1300, the radio reported the three craters had grown tremendously. Black clouds of pumice and steam from the boiling sea rose ten to fifteen thousand feet. Fortunately, it drifted northeast away from the island due to prevailing winds. The ground continued to shake violently as far as three hundred meters from the fissure. Molten lava was blown out of the craters in huge globs and was reaching out further and further toward town. Firefighting in a shower of molten lava was impossible. On the eastern part of town, the few remaining rescue workers and a selected group of male residents were brought back to the island. They emptied/stripped the homes of their contents as much as possible. They had two trucks to move the possessions to warehouses near the harbor. Cars were ferried to the mainland.

Below is a newspaper photo that appeared in the local press on the twenty-third (See figure 4).

Figure 4. Photo of burnt-out home on 24 January

Early in the day, one of the homes was ignited by a shower of molten lava and burnt to the ground. By nightfall, one house had been destroyed, five were encircled with lava flow, and twenty more were in danger. Fallout from the volcano was being reported across the island and was being detected even along the southern coast. Farmers in that area were warned to feed their livestock indoors due to the danger of poisoning from noxious gases in the pumice. The below photo taken from a postcard shows the cloud on the twenty-fourth (See figure 5).

Figure 5. Taken from mainland on 24 January.

By midday on the twenty fourth, volcanologists, geologists, geophysicists, physicists, seismologists, and engineers from the mainland were assessing the damage. The initial conclusion was that it was a standard fissure eruption of minimum magma yield. It was "to last only a few months." They called it a "minor eruption." They were a bit troubled by the water temperature in the city wells that were six hundred meters deep and yielding very hot water.

It was on the second day after seeing all the press coverage on the television that my family and I drove along the southern coast of Iceland and photographed the eruption from afar. That was my first glimpse of an active volcanic eruption. I was impressed with Thor's "mighty hammer."

When I showed the back cover photo to some Icelanders, they immediately showed me the "face of Thor" in the volcanic cloud.

DAY THREE: 25 JANUARY

By the morning of the twenty-fifth, the three main craters were actively flowing lava to the east. A new peninsula had been formed that was eight hundred meters long and six hundred meters wide. The harbor entrance was getting smaller.

Here's a photo taken from a postcard that shows what things looked like on the evening of the twenty-fifth (See figure 6).

Figure 6. Photo of the only harbor and the volcano on 25 January

BATTLING THOR

Reefer ships were brought in, and they began to load fresh frozen fish. Another ship was loading salted fish. For a two-hour period, the detail was interrupted due to east winds bringing pumice and cinder over the town. As a side note, the island had four fish-freezing plants. They handled 12,700 tons of fresh frozen cod in 1972. Normally, anywhere from eighty-five to ninety fishing boats operated from the harbor each winter. They brought in twenty-five thousand metric tons of cod, haddock, and related species and eighty thousand tons of capelin. Fishing and the use of the harbor was their life, and they were fighting to preserve it.

The below photo from the local paper shows the activity in the harbor on the third evening (Figure 7).

Figure 7. Chaos in the harbor during the evacuation

DAYS FOUR AND FIVE: 26-27 JANUARY

Sveinn Erickson, Fire Chief of Keflavík Airport, was designated as the head of the Civil Defense effort on the island. Here is a picture of Sveinn shortly after he arrived on the island (See figure 8).

Figure 8. Photo of Sveinn Erickson, Director of the Civil Defense effort

Sveinn requested aircraft support from the NATO base to rescue a rare breed of sheep found only on that island. Two Dakota aircraft and helicopters were used to evacuate the 399 sheep by the end of the day on the twenty-seventh (See figure 9).

Figure 9. Newspaper clipping with interpreter's notes.

Sveinn also requested that the US Defense Force supply him with a high-pressure pump truck that pumped two thousand liters of water per minute. He was intending to divert the lava flow by cooling the lava nearest the town. Furniture boxes and asbestos suits good to six hundred degrees centigrade were also requested and supplied. Local chaplains on base started a clothing drive and delivered over one ton of clothing to the distribution center in Reykjavík. Five US aircraft were put on standby to respond to emergency calls. The Commanding Officer of the Ground Defense Force in Keflavík pledged to further support the Icelandic government with additional equipment and people. This was how I entered the support effort. I was the Officer in-Charge of the *Flugbjörgunarsveitin í Keflavík* (the Air-Ground Searching Team of Keflavik).

The island of Heimaey was declared off-limits to all but residents. The Icelandic press was not happy, especially after foreign journalists snuck to Heimaey by renting a boat. Shortly thereafter, permission was granted for all press to go to the island, but they were placed under strict control.

EUGENE DALE SCHWARTZLOW

This photo of Heimaey on the twenty-seventh was extracted from a postcard. It shows a very distinct cone had been formed in just four days (See figure 10).

Figure 10. The harbor and volcano on 27 January

While all this activity was going on, the press and the politicians were doing battle. Questions such as, "Why not remove all Americans living off-base from their housing so they could provide the displaced islanders with housing?"; "Should they request foreign government support to aid the effort?"; and "Can the islanders handle this crisis on their own?" were being raised. On the thirtieth, the newspaper *Morgunblaðið* reported that the people of Iceland were upset that the government didn't accept the United States' offer to help right away. The pride and prejudices of the politicians were contrary to the wishes of the general population. Eventually, Sveinn could request American and Nordic assistance. While they were talking, ash was blowing across town with an unfavorable

BATTLING THOR

wind and accumulating as much as eight feet of ash an hour. Red-hot cinders were landing on roofs or breaking windows and lighting the homes on fire.

A local paper carried this photo (See figure 11).

Figure 11. Another burnt-out home caused by red-hot embers from the volcano.

The Icelanders began boarding up windows on the sides of homes facing the volcano and shoveling ash off the roof, but they were having trouble getting organized and getting the work done. It was clear from the press coverage that they needed assistance.

DAYS SIX THROUGH TEN:
28 JANUARY TO 1 FEBRUARY

By 30 January, one hundred and fifty homes had been destroyed by lava and fire, and many homes were buried. The extract from the local paper and my interpreter's notes are shown below See figure 12).

Figure 12. The ash covered town on 30 January.

The article went on to say that the Icelandic civil service workforce, made up mostly of college student volunteers, was disorganized and ineffective. On 31 January, the newspaper *Vísir* reported that the Icelandic people were unwilling to evict Americans from their homes if they lived off-base. It was at that point that the US SAR team was requested to assist Sveinn Erickson on the island. The Commanding Officer of the Naval Station in Keflavík requested a leader and one hundred men. I was the first to volunteer to lead the team. A Reykjavík newspaper showed Icelanders discussing what needs to be done (See figure 13).

BATTLING THOR

Figure 13. A meeting of the Civil Defense leaders

AMERICAN SEARCH AND RESCUE TEAM CALLED UP

DAY ELEVEN: 2 FEBRUARY

Early on the second, myself, fifty enlisted Marines from Marine Barracks Iceland, twenty-five sailors from the Naval Station, and twenty-five air force enlisted from COMFAIR Keflavík were enroute to the island via a Dakota aircraft. We carried a waterproof bag of clothing and four days of military C rations. I and the senior enlisted men wore orange jumpsuits. Our workers all had red/orange vests for ease of recognition. The only communications equipment we had was some old AN/PRC-6 handheld radios with only a few batteries. They were useless.

The pilot made a point of flying around the island prior to landing. Even in the predawn light, it was a spectacular sight (See figure 14).

Figure 14. Our first predawn view of the volcano as we flew to the airfield.

It was a bit eerie, and the fear of the unknown was building (See figure 15).

BATTLING THOR

Figure 15. Our approach to the island

Our first real view of the cone was impressive. The realization that this was just a flat stretch of farmland a few days earlier was unbelievable.

Looking though the aircraft window made it rather surreal, because we couldn't hear the rumbles and roars of the explosions (See figure 16).

Figure 16. The volcano as seen from the aircraft.

Even though there was a well-developed cone, the fissure line was still visible (See figure 17).

Figure18. The fissure line

For the moment, the ash was blowing away from town (See figure 19).

Figure 19. View from the aircraft

Some hot spots were more aggressive than others (See figure 20).

Figure 20. The fissure at the edge of Heimay

EUGENE DALE SCHWARTZLOW

For all of us on the aircraft, it was an exciting time as we made our final approach, and we could see the active volcano just a short distance from the runway. We all got a bit concerned when our aircraft hit a down draft caused by the hot air columns from the volcano. Our aircraft dropped an estimated three hundred feet in just seconds. Everyone's stomachs felt like they were near their earlobes. In just a few moments, we were on the ground and reporting for duty (See figure 21).

Figure 21. Our aircraft on the runway

I was briefed by Sveinn that the priority of our work effort was to be to try to remove as much ash as we could from the homes to prevent further roof collapse.

At that point, there was no long-range plan, and we had no idea where we would be sleeping that evening.

As the Joint Task Force Commander, I immediately headed to high ground to assess the situation and plan my work details.

BATTLING THOR

Figure 22. Captain Schwartzlow on a roof top assessing the damage.

19

EUGENE DALE SCHWARTZLOW

My right-hand man was Chief Morgan, a superb Seabee! Once again, the Seabees and Marines were working together for the common good (See figure 23).

Figure 23. Seabee Chief Morgan

BATTLING THOR

I had one staff NCO assigned to each of the twenty-five-man platoons. Each platoon was further organized into six four-man teams. It was with this basic organization that we dispatched "house details" to accomplish our mission. This photo shows some of the men on their first roof (See figure 24).

Figure 24 Two teams having a lunch break on a roof.

EUGENE DALE SCHWARTZLOW

The work we accomplished on the first day was somewhat limited. Much of the day was spent getting to the island and getting set up. However, by nightfall, we had cleared ash from thirty homes. Here is one of the official navy photos taken on that first day (See figure 25).

Figure 25. Two sailors shoveling ash from the roof.

We also had one emergency project. The roof of the new hospital was about to collapse from the weight of all the scoria. In an all-hands effort, we moved six thousand tons of material from the roof in four hours. We didn't have any ladders, so a nearby crane became our ladder (See figure 26).

Figure 26. Two Marines climbing to the roof top via the crane.

With all one hundred men working on the roof of a hospital, it didn't take long to finish the job (See figure 27).

Figure 27. Shoveling ash off a hospital

EUGENE DALE SCHWARTZLOW

A NIGHT AT SEA

As the day progressed and the winds shifted to the east, it became apparent there was no safe place for my workforce to rest overnight. The red-hot missiles became more and more prevalent, and the danger of getting hit in the head with rocks or getting blinded was increasing. I put out an urgent plea to the defense force to provide helmets and goggles for day two.

Around 2000 hours, we were told to muster at the harbor. There was a fishing boat waiting to take us off the island.

Here is a shot of what we saw as we left the harbor (See figure 28).

Figure 28. View of the volcano from our boat in the harbor.

Seeing the actual flow as it worked its way to the sea was interesting. The volcano was really shaped like a horseshoe with an open end.

Once we cleared the harbor, we pulled up alongside a cruise ship. The seas were rough. The sailors lashed the ship and the boat together, and I was told to transfer people and equipment to the ship. The boat was heaving up and down as we attempted to make the transfer. There were no safety lines and no connecting gangway, and the only way to get from boat to ship was to wait until the boat peaked and leap into the awaiting arms of two large Icelanders. I was sure we would have someone miscalculate and be crushed between the crafts (See figure 29).

Figure 29. At sea transfer of men and equipment

Although the photos are of poor quality, they show the chaos and danger associated with strapping a small fishing boat to a cruise ship in the rough seas (See figure 30).

Figure 30. It was a leap of faith.

EUGENE DALE SCHWARTZLOW

A total of 102 people jumped for their life, and 102 made it. Only one shovel fell to its death. By the time this high-sea adventure was over, the small boat had broken many of the portholes and creased the cruise ship in multiple places. God was watching over us that night. Once aboard, we were treated to a great meal and a good night's sleep.

DAY TWELVE: 3 FEBRUARY

We returned to the harbor in the morning and disembarked from the fishing boat at about 0800. The winds were favorable. We were clearly organized for business. We set up our headquarters in the community center with maps and project listings. In the picture below, I identify those houses to be worked on by the various teams (See figure 21).

Figure 21. I mapped out the area to be worked.

Below is the map I made up for the second day of operations (See figure 22).

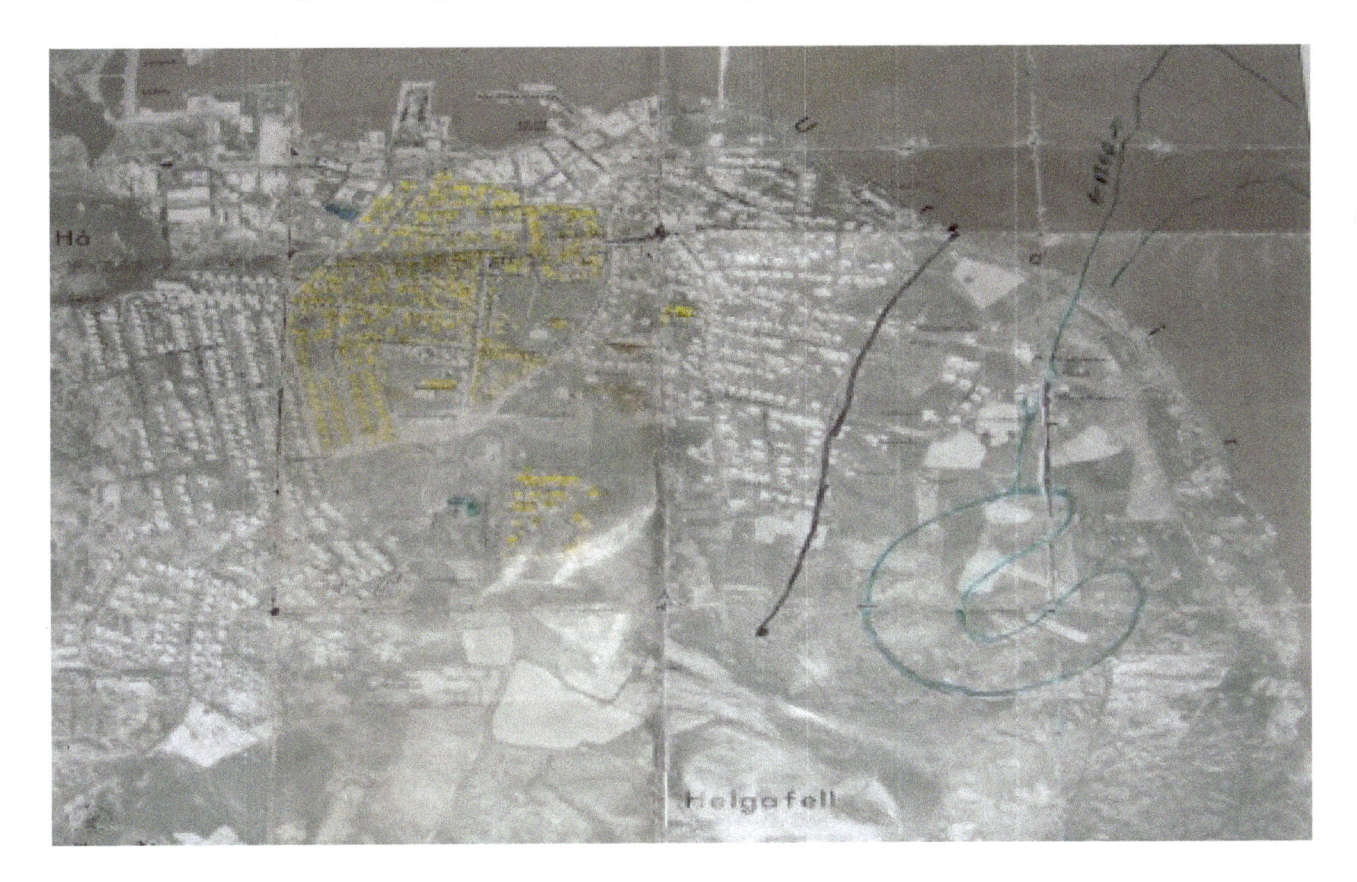

Figure 22. Our working map

My navy yeoman assisted in keeping our project board up to date (See figure 23).

Figure 23. The project board lists all tasks to be performed.

He also maintained the area map. The below map shows the basic flow of the lava, and the blue line shows the boundary of no-man's-land, where everything was already destroyed. If you look to the lower left, you can see where our initial command post (CP) was located (See figure 24).

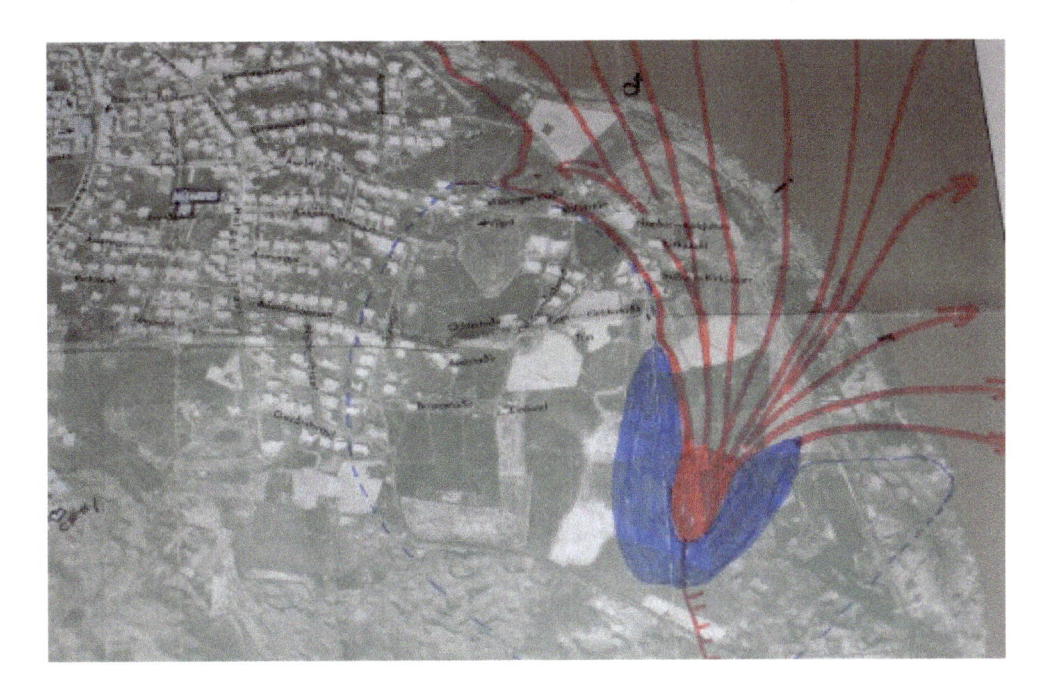

Figure 24. Our master map shows lava flow and forward edge of buried homes.

During the second day, Chief Morgan had located a vehicle in the scoria, and we were given permission to use it as a command vehicle. It wasn't pretty, but it did the job (See figure 25).

Figure 25. Chief Morgan in our "Command Vehicle".

Having a vehicle made supervision of the workforce a lot easier.

Once we had wheels, we could get out and see the challenges from various perspectives. One of the first things we noticed was that the scoria was eight to twenty feet deep and packed well enough that we could drive on it (See figure 26).

Figure 26. A city street after an hour of falling ash.

The volcano was quiet on our second day, as you can see by the below photograph (See figure 27).

Figure 27. The volcano viewed from downtown.

On the left of the below picture, you can just barely see a vehicle that is buried in the scoria (See figure 28).

Figure 28. Cars covered with ash.

Below is a view of the ash buildup on one of the roofs looking toward the harbor (See figure 29).

Figure 29. Looking toward the harbor from a roof top.

It was hard to believe that ash could fall at such an alarming rate that an entire town could be buried in just a few hours (See figure 30).

Figure 30. The ash we were removing from the roofs.

Vehicles were buried all along the streets. Staying in the middle of the road was pure guesswork (See figure 31).

Figure 31. Driving on the scoria was not a problem.

My insistence that all my supervisors wear orange jumpsuits and the workers wear safety vests paid off. All I had to do to see who was working was to go to high ground and look for them on the roofs.

Here's a crew working on a home (please note that the windows have been boarded up or covered with corrugated tin to prevent red-hot rocks from entering the home (See figure 32).

Figure 32. A four-man crew clearing a roof.

Favorable winds blew the scoria away from the town, so these two teams could remove the ash (See figure 33).

Figure 33. Shoveling ash while the volcano roared.

This is how that area looked once I stepped back a bit further (See figure 34).

Figure 34. Working under dangerous conditions

Note the Marine Staff NCOs are in their SAR jumpsuits (See figure 35).

Figure 35. Workers and supervisors

BATTLING THOR

Our lunches consisted of military C rations for the first few days. Here, the troops are enjoying lunch on a rooftop overlooking the volcano. The photograph does not do justice to the real situation that they all faced. The volcano roared and the ground shook each time the volcano "burped." This continued every minute of every day that we were on the island. It was as if we were fighting the mighty Thor, God of Thunder (See figure 36).

Figure 36. Lunch break below the cone.

In this picture, three different crews can be seen working on three separate roofs (See figure 37).

Figure 37. Three crews clearing ash off the roofs.

By the end of the day, we had shoveled out doorways and cleared the roofs of 110 homes. Ladders were in short supply, so the teams had to get creative (See figure 38).

Figure 38. One ladder, two floors.

Later that day, I conducted a short awards ceremony for several of the men on one of the rooftops (See figure 39).

BATTLING THOR

Figure 39. Awards ceremony on a roof top

In the late afternoon, I stopped by the forward edge of the lava flow to check on the harbor (See figure 40).

Figure 40. The lava flow into the harbor

EUGENE DALE SCHWARTZLOW

The molten lava meeting the sea sent clouds of steam into the air. The faster the lava flowed, the more steam. It became a good indicator of the amount of flow each day (See figure 41).

Figure 41. Captain "S" checking out the lava encroachment into the harbor.

At two thousand degrees Fahrenheit, it was hard to stand very close to the wall, even with protective clothing (See figure 42).

Figured 42. Ever moving hot lava

BATTLING THOR

Nearby, an Icelandic policeman was extracting lava and pressing coins into the center of the molten rock (Figure 43).

Figure 43. Policeman pushing a coin into molten lava.

I later borrowed his shovel and made three souvenirs of my own (See figure 44):

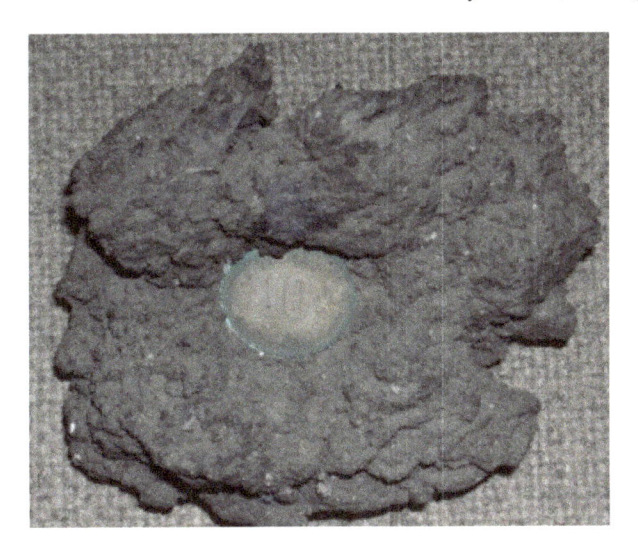

Figure 44. *Kronur* in basalt

EUGENE DALE SCHWARTZLOW

After I got the troops bedded down, I and two SNCOs decided to hike up Helgafell, the five-thousand-year-old volcano that looked down into the growing volcano. By this time, it was one large volcano. When we got to the top of the old volcano, the view was spectacular, and the heat was very noticeable. The wind was blowing the heat away, and it was still very uncomfortable.

I shot multiple pictures of the volcano (See figure 45).

Figure 45. Observing the eruptions

From on top of the old volcano, we had a great view looking in (See figure 46).

Figure 46. Looking into the crater from Helgafell

Zooming in made it look even more spectacular (See figure 47).

At times, the height of the blasts was enormous. We had the constant desire to get closer, even if it was only via telephoto lens (See figure 48).

Figure 48. Explosion reaching high into the night sky.

Once we returned to ground level, there were two distinct areas of eruption as shown in this photo (See figure 49).

Figure 49. Two hot spots

Even the Icelandic horse seems to rise out of the cone (See figure 50).

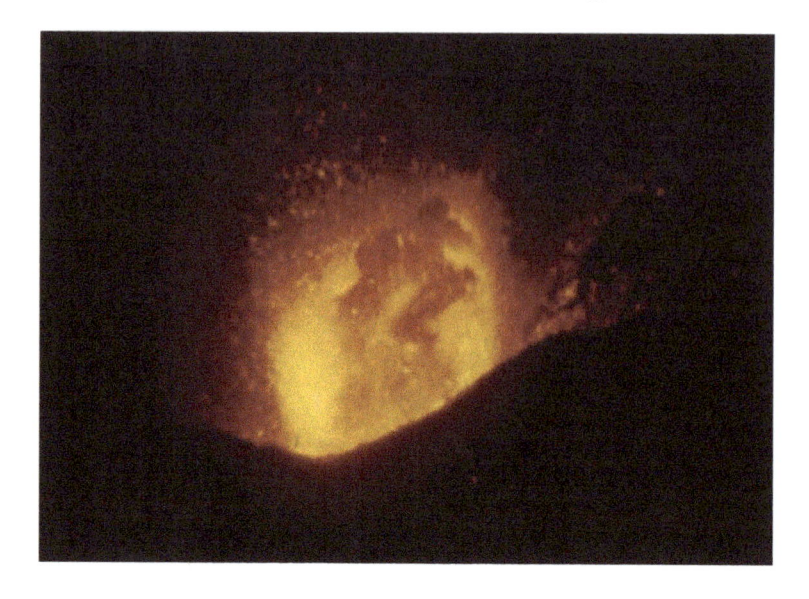

Figure 50. Thor's Icelandic horses

Later that night, I sent a note to the mainland. I informed them, "Personnel going to the island to work in the future are encouraged to bring helmets, goggles, Icelandic socks and gloves, a spare pair of boots, and enough clothes to last at least a week. Long underwear is a necessity. It also is important for married personnel to explain to their wives that they may be on the island for as much as a week or two because of the possibility of bad weather."

We slept in the community center that evening.

DAY THIRTEEN: 4 FEBRUARY

Part of my workforce was rotated out on 4 February. I kept fifty Marines and twenty-five airmen and sailors as my workforce.

Sveinn continued to have men push up the scoria to form a wall in hopes that it would divert the flow of the lava and save the harbor and town (See figure 51).

Figure 51. The manmade berm

Once the wall was pushed up, it looked like this (See figure 52).

Figure 52. The completed berm with lava on the rise.

They also continued to sprinkle water on the lava flow with the fire hoses (See figure 53).

Figure 53. An attempt to cool the forward edge of the lava.

BATTLING THOR

There was much debate about the success of that effort.
With the recent snowfall, the view of the volcano from town took on an all-new look (See figure 54).

Figure 54. The eruption above the snow-covered town.

Early on, I was tasked to do daily drives to report to Admiral Behling my assessment of the dangers, problems, and logistic matters. This assessment included checking the original fault line. Here, I am on my first visit to the original fault line that had since cooled down (See figure 55).

Figure 55. The view of the original fault line after it had cooled down.

45

Below is a close-up of the rocks along the fault line. The yellow rocks were ones coated by the escaping sulfur gases. The red rocks were pumice (See figure 56).

Figure 56. Pumice and basalt covered with sulfur.

On several occasions, Chief Hicks and I were called upon to pick up rock samples for geologists. We also gathered a few for our own personal souvenirs. Here is a photo of Chief Hicks along the fault line (See figure 57).

Figure 57. Hicks exploring the fault line.

BATTLING THOR

Chief Hicks and Capt S picking up rock samples (See Figure 58 & 59).

Figure 58. Chief Hicks gathers basalt samples.

Figure 59. Capt. S gathers sulfur coated pumice.

EUGENE DALE SCHWARTZLOW

Shown are two of the rock samples I gathered. The red was pumice. The black rock was very heavy. It was mainly basalt (See figure 60 & 61).

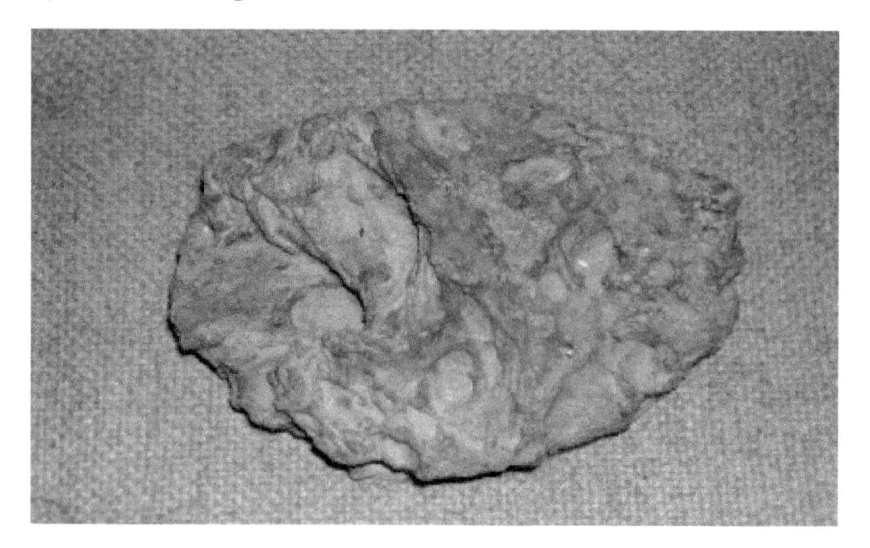

Figure 60. Pumice

Figure 61. Basalt

I was also asked to observe the advancement of the lava flow toward town and into the harbor. Here are some of the views we had (See figures 62 through 65).

BATTLING THOR

Figure 62. The forward wall.

Figure 63. The incredible heat—1200 degrees Centigrade

EUGENE DALE SCHWARTZLOW

Figure 64. The slow moving forward edge.

Figure 65. The lava flow reached the telephone pole.

The entry of the lava into the harbor didn't present much of a problem at first.

BATTLING THOR

As it progressed, the concern grew that the harbor would be lost (See figure 66.

Figure 66. The harbor is getting smaller.

The view up close made it seem even more helpless (See figure 67).

Figure 67. The steady flow of lava into the harbor.

The harbor entrance was getting smaller (See figure 68).

Figure 68. The harbor entrance is getting narrow.

By day's end, we had shoveled the roofs of fifty houses and cleared the large roofs of five businesses.

Along with the incoming personnel came a crate of goggles and helmets. The Icelanders provided the helmets. What a hoot! There were campaign helmets from World War I and II, German helmets, search and rescue helmets, and everything in between. All of them afforded a reasonable amount of protection from the red-hot cinders. It did make my workforce look like they were from *Hogan's Heroes*.

That evening, I received a call from CBS News in the States. They were live and wanted my assessment of what I was seeing and experiencing. I told them that all media was to go through the naval station's public affairs officer. The caller insisted. He then asked, "Looking out your window, what do you see?" I responded, "Boards and corrugated aluminum; the windows are all boarded shut, because the red-hot cinders were breaking windows and setting houses on fire." He then reminded me that we were on live television. I then reminded him he wasn't supposed to call me.

DAY FOURTEEN: 5 FEBRUARY

We were better equipped for this day's activities. We dug out many vehicles, found some rope, and rigged ash dredges to pull across the roofs (See figure 69).

Figure 69. Getting the job done with heavy equipment.

The crew rigged sleds, which helped to move ash off the roofs more rapidly (See figure 70).

Figure 70. A crew working smarter, not harder.

We had learned the hard way that we should not remove all the scoria from the roofs. A two-inch layer of cinder/scoria left on the roof insulated it from the red-hot rocks that fell nearly every day.

EUGENE DALE SCHWARTZLOW

By evening, we had cleared 183 homes and removed seven pallets of fish from a fish factory that had collapsed (See figure 71).

Figure 71. Ash removal was continued on the roofs of the homes.

DAY FIFTEEN: 6 FEBRUARY

6 February was a busy day. We had added a few new tasks. First, we boxed up and evacuated the private property of ten homes. Second, we shoveled ash off thirty roofs. Third, we were called upon to clear the ash from two large fish factories. Fourth, we shoveled off the roofs of five large businesses. Sixth, we cleared six doorways, which were now under ten to twelve feet of scoria. Seventh, we cleaned off the roof of the local high school. Eighth, we surveyed an x-ray machine that needed to be moved.

At about noon, while my workers were taking a lunch break, I was informed we could no longer eat in the harbor mess hall. The levels of sulfur, methane, and other gases like CO_2 were getting too high. They were so high that many vehicles driving through the area stalled because there was not enough oxygen to support combustion. They asked me to move my workforce and support infrastructure to the school sitting on the high ground away from the volcano. We did so, and by early afternoon, were relocated and back doing the mission.

Our last task took us late into the night evacuating contents of a fish factory that was about to be consumed by the lava flow. We were working under temporary lighting for the entire night as the lava slowly crept forward. We evacuated eighteen million kroner worth of salted fish from the factory. The building was stripped of machinery. Sixty tons of fish were removed. We finally finished at about 0200. Shown here is the crew lifting pallets of fish through a hole in the roof (See figure 72).

Figure 72. Hauling out pallets of fish through a hole in the roof.

As we started to work, the lava was rapidly approaching the building. For some unknown reason, the lava stopped its movement for a few hours, giving us time to rescue the contents of the building (See figure 73).

Figure 73. The fish factory is being kissed by the lava wall.

EUGENE DALE SCHWARTZLOW

Two days later, I stopped by to see how far the lava had advanced and witnessed the final destruction of the factory (See figure 74).

Figure 74. Lava overtakes the Fish Factory

Earlier that day, I was making my rounds of the area, and I saw a demolished house sticking out rather precariously from a wall of advancing scoria and lava. Much to my surprise, a man emerged from a broken doorway carrying his toilet bowl. I couldn't believe that he had been in there (See figure 75).

Figure 75. The home the man emerged from with his toilet bowl.

BATTLING THOR

During the day of 6 February, there was a significant event happening in the harbor. Although the Icelanders feared the advancing lava had closed the harbor, they were unsure. One brave fisherman brought in his load of fish and unloaded his catch. He was a signal to many that there was hope. As you can see, the lava looks like it is closing the harbor "door". However, by hugging the far bank, the boat had plenty of water to enter the harbor (See figures 76 & 77),

Figure 76. The boat approaching the harbor.

Figure 77. The boat enters the harbor.

As you can see, the boat is loaded down with capelin (See figure 78).

Figure 78. A boat loaded with fish.

Once they got to the pier side, they commenced off-loading the fish (See figure 79). It was a good day's catch and uplifting to all who saw this significant event. It offered hope.

Figure 79. Off-loading a catch of capelin.

DAY SIXTEEN: 7 FEBRUARY
On the seventh, it was time for another troop rotation. They flew in by C-117s. See figure 80.

Figure 80. C-117 has landed.

After we got the new folks settled in, we gave them their assignments and put them to work. They cleared four large factory roofs and responded to three emergency house projects, and twenty-two men moved furniture for the rest of the day.

DAY SEVENTEEN: 8 FEBRUARY
On the eighth, the tasks we received from Sveinn showed we were making progress. We were asked to dig out twelve fuel tanks so they could restore heating to several areas. We moved a lot of furniture. We had only a few roof projects. We crated and removed an x-ray machine (See figure 81).

Figure 81. Saving an X-ray machine

EUGENE DALE SCHWARTZLOW

We responded to one emergency request to dig out the local blacksmith's house and shop. Throughout the day, we had a crew who dug out, repaired, and/or towed vehicles from the ash filled streets. At this point, many of the easternmost streets were under thirty feet of ash, and the homes that were early victims of the volcano were visible only as slight dips in the sea of scoria. Here's a photograph of Chief Morgan as he inspects the damage (See figure 82).

Figure 82. Chief Morgan on the roof tops

Here's another view of the scoria buildup (See figure 83).

Figure 83. Cleared roofs and scoria build up in the field.

60

DAY EIGHTEEN: 9 FEBRUARY

The ninth was filled with multiple tasks. We loaded furniture into CONEX boxes. We hauled garbage, which was becoming a new problem. We picked up furniture and loaded over 18,000 lb. of cargo in a DC-6 aircraft. We dug out the doors to the new hospital. The rest of the day was spent digging out more vehicles.

DAY NINETEEN: 10 FEBRUARY

We turned over only two teams. The airfield was closed due to bad weather. As can be seen by this photo of our headquarters/school, the visibility was poor, and the freezing temperatures and snow with high winds made working more difficult (See figure 84).

Figure 84. Our schoolhouse home during a snowstorm

Despite that, our US sanitation team worked with the Icelandic police on various projects, a SEAL team conducted an underwater beach survey, and we loaded 20,000 lb. of cargo on the DC-6. We also cleared 293 doorways to allow work crews in. Five teams carried goods and furniture. One team shoveled off a large fish factory. One team searched for the peaks of houses and responded to two emergency calls for shoveling off houses.

By the end of the day, with strong volcanic activity, the local paper announced that the island was 1½ square kilometers larger than it had been prior to the eruption.

EUGENE DALE SCHWARTZLOW

DAY TWENTY: 11 FEBRUARY

Day by day, our work crew tasks became more difficult. On the eleventh, we removed two tractors from a factory roof using a crane we had found. We cleared 325 doorways. We dug out nine oil tanks with a backhoe to allow heating to take place. Twenty-one men moved goods and furniture. Pictured here is a crew loading furniture into the aircraft from CONEX boxes (See figure 85).

Figure 85. Loading furniture on aircraft

We continued to move large numbers of vehicles to the storage compound. Our sheet metal workers made ash hoods for the town's chimneys.

Fortunately for us, the volcano was relatively quiet that day, and winds blew the scoria away from town (See figure 86).

Figure 86. A quiet day. A day to work.

DAY TWENTY-ONE: 12 FEBRUARY

We cleared 306 doorways, dug out eleven oil filters, shoveled twelve roofs, dug out and moved a lumberyard, prepared 110 chimney lids, completed the rolling stock inventory, continued to work with the IPs on sanitation matters, and removed furniture from sixty houses. C-130s were brought in to move large quantities of personal effects (See figure 87).

Figure 87. C-130's on the runway.

As time went on, snow slowed the property evacuation due to runway conditions (See figure 88).

Figure 88. Backup of property awaiting aircraft

THE TURNOVER

My replacement, Marine Captain Steve Mychinski, arrived on the afternoon of the twelfth. I was very tired and ready to see my family. By the time I left, we had run the full gamut of living accommodations. We had stayed aboard ship, in a community center, and in two schools. The below map shows where the three headquarters buildings were located (See figure 89).

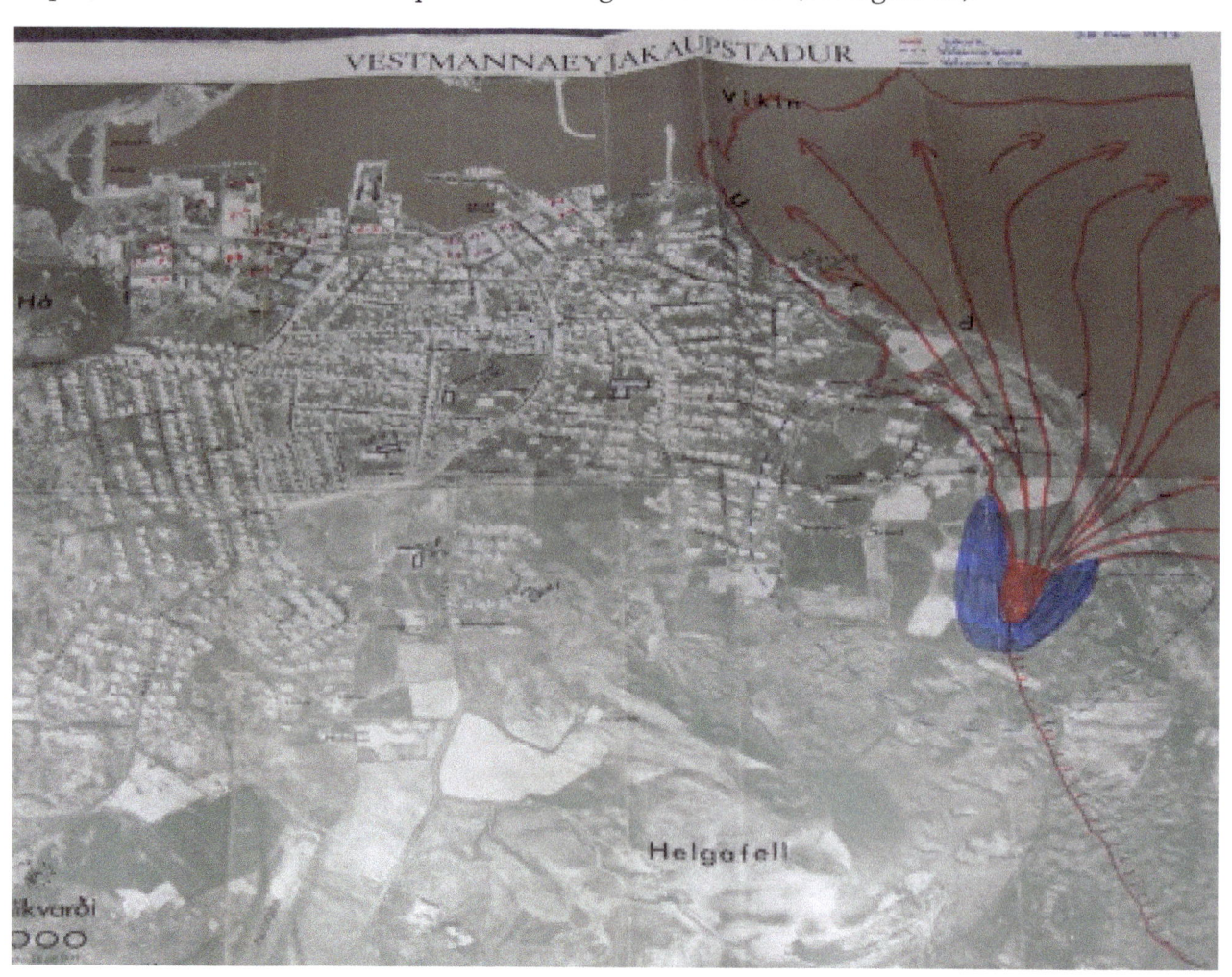

Figure 89. City map with lodging locations noted.

By the time Steve got to the island, we were living in the new addition of the elementary school house. Showers, heating, and lighting were all available. All personnel received two hot meals a day

BATTLING THOR

in the Icelandic mess hall. The volcano had settled down to the extent that the personnel working was no longer in danger from either lava flow or the red-hot falling ash (See figure 90).

Figure 90. The "sleeping giant" on 12 February.

For the remainder of the day on the twelfth, Steve and I toured the island so I could get him snapped into his new job. We visited the lava flow and the harbor for a final look (See figure 91).

Figure 91. Steve on the cooled forward edge of the lava flow

65

EUGENE DALE SCHWARTZLOW

The flow continued to move as Steve climbed back down (See figure 92).

Figure 92. Captain "M" on the lava wall

I then took him to the edge of no-man's-land (See figure 93).

Figure 93. The forward wall

BATTLING THOR

We then walked up Helgafell for a look into the volcano. I was surprised to see that the new cone was now higher than the top of Helgafell.

Here's a series of shots taken that night. The view looking into the horseshoe-shaped volcano was quite unique (See figure 94 through 109).

Figure 94

Even several hundred feet away, the heat was intense.

Figure 95

EUGENE DALE SCHWARTZLOW

Basalt rocks as large as houses were rolling down the slopes. The ground shook with every spectacular burst.

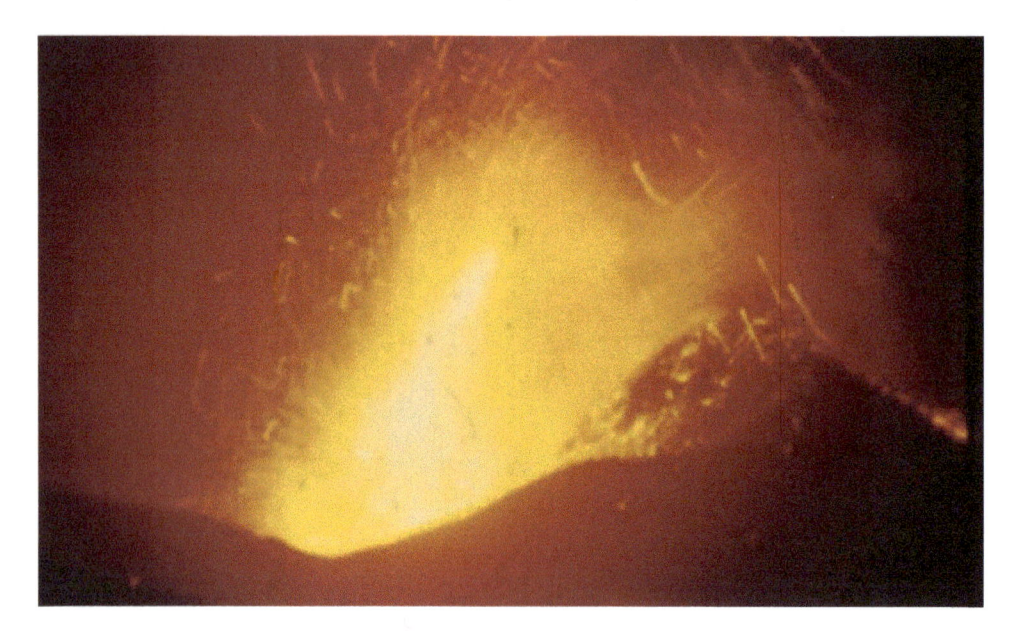

Figure 96

As I changed the camera filter, the explosions took on a new appearance.

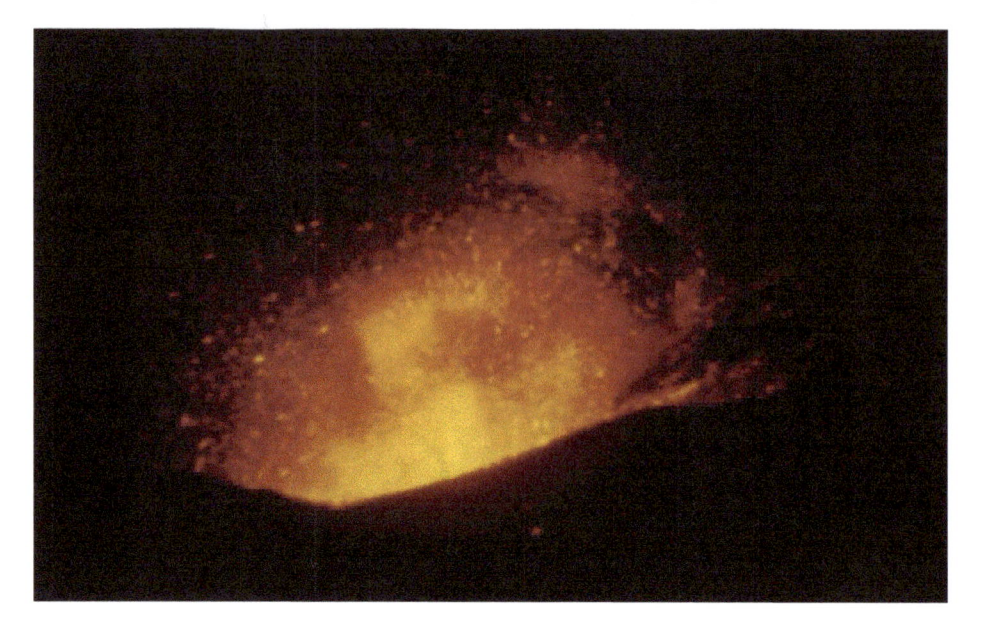

Figure 97

BATTLING THOR

No two photographs were the same. It was like watching an endless chain of fireworks. My favorite photo taken that night appears below. It was like looking into the mouth of hell.

Figure 98

The flames jumped hundreds of feet high from explosions thirty-five miles below the surface. We could have watched for hours. As a matter of fact, I guess we did.

Figure 99

Fortunately for us, the wind was blowing away from Helgafell.

Figure 100

The lower we hiked, the higher the flames seemed to rise.

Figure 101

BATTLING THOR

Double simultaneous eruptions were common.

Figure 102

Regardless, they all revealed an unbelievable view.

Figure 103

Zooming in to capture the quantity of huge rocks flying over the rim was tried repeatedly.

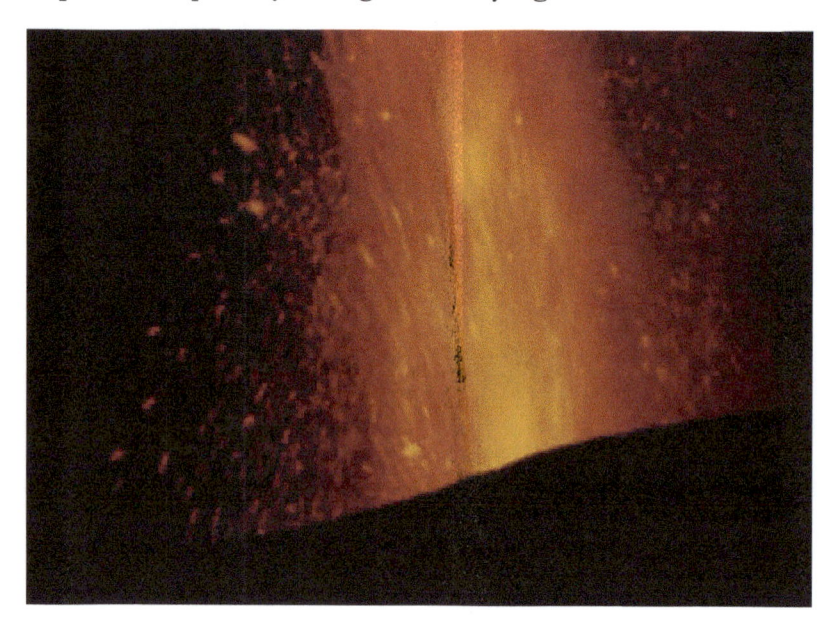

Figure 104.

Staring into the inferno was even more compelling than staring into the flames of a campfire.

Figure 105

BATTLING THOR

It was hard to comprehend that I was watching the birth of land.

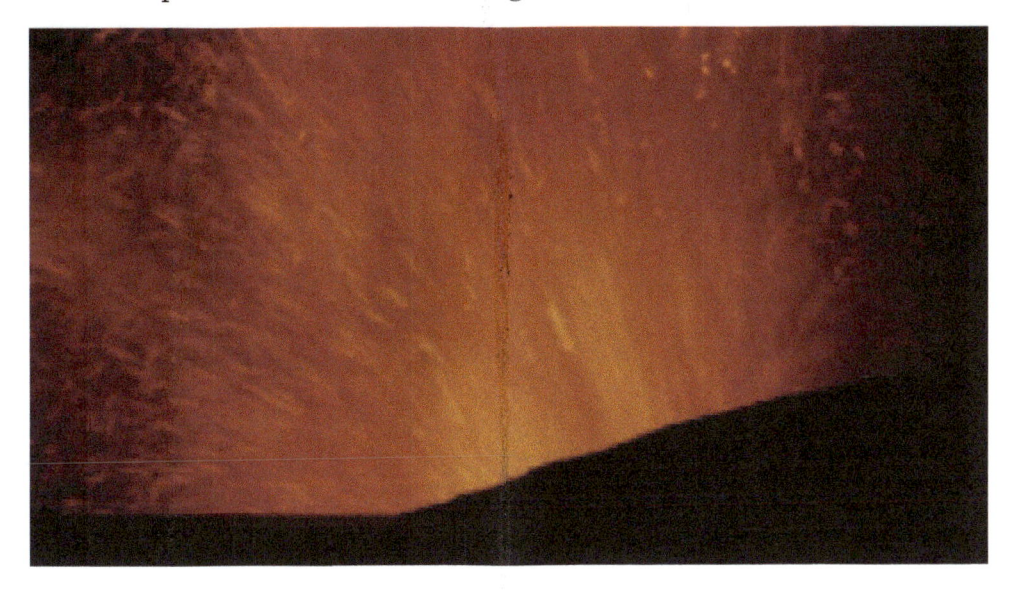

Figure 106

Up close or observing from afar, watching the earth's surface changing before our eyes was a wonder to behold.

Figure 107

EUGENE DALE SCHWARTZLOW

Looking into the caldron was a memory I'll never forget.

Figure 108

Our last look was from the churchyard at the base of *Helgafeld*, looking back up at the cone.

Figure 109

RETURNING HOME

DAY TWENTY-TWO: 13 FEBRUARY

I departed Heimaey at first light on the thirteenth and arrived at Keflavík, Iceland shortly thereafter.

Early on the thirteenth, I was called into the Armed Forces Radio and TV studio for a live interview. I was very tired but managed to answer their questions and to give everyone a feeling of what it was like.

POST-OPERATION REFLECTIONS

In addition to the day-by-day activities that I mentioned previously, there were several other events that I experienced that offered leadership challenges to us during our stay. I no longer recall the exact date that these events occurred, but all of them remain locked in my memory.

GUIDED TOURS FOR VIPS

Visitor control was one of my many jobs each day. I hosted Marine Barracks Sergeant Major Ewing and Captain McDonald (CO of Naval Station). Each was given a tour of the area. Sergeant Major Ewing's visit was uneventful, but Captain McDonald's visit was a bit too exciting.

The sergeant major was my first visitor. I had been on the island several days, and the volcano had settled down a bit by then. I first took him out to the original rift line above the town (See figure 110).

Figure 110. Sergeant Major Ewing at the watering berm.

Then we went out to "no-man's-land" (See figure 111).

BATTLING THOR

Figure 111. Sergeant Major alongside of a 30-foot power pole

One of the roof peaks is just barely visible (See figure 112).

Figure 112. The view of the town from "No man's land".

Captain McDonald and his party were particularly interested in the harbor and the volcano itself. Here we are at the harbor (See Figure 113).

Figure 113. VIPs looking at the harbor.

As you can see, our transportation was upgraded to a land rover for the captain (See figure 114).

Figure 114. Inspecting party and their jeep

Here, the captain is observing the lava flow (See figure 115).

Figure 115. VIPs up close to the advancing lava wall

The visitors also toured no-man's-land (See figure 116).

Figure 116. No Man's Land—homes we could not save.

When I took the group to see the original fissure that had closed, there was snow on the ground. I cautioned him that he should only walk where the snow was not melted. All other areas were potentially dangerous. I didn't take my own advice. As I was saying this, my foot broke through the earth's crust, and there, one foot below me, was molten lava. We all did a hasty retreat, and I did not go back to that spot again (See figure 117).

Figure 117. Walking along the original fault line

IMPROPER REQUEST

After I had been battling the volcano for a few days, I received an envelope from my mainland point of contact, Colonel T. of the US Army. In the envelope were several self-addressed envelopes. I was asked by the colonel to go to the locked post office and manually cancel each of the envelopes with the date of the eruption: 23 January 1973. I could not believe it. I had been asked by a senior officer to break into the post office and do something improper. I then wrote a note back to the colonel and told him I could not do what he asked. I reminded him of the astronauts that had done such things for personal gain and how much trouble they got into hitting golf balls. I in turn notified my Marine boss, Major Dick Wiedner, and Captain McDonald. No one said anything to me about this further.

THE THIEF

The third day on the island presented a new leadership challenge. That night, one of the sailor's broke curfews and was caught stealing in one of the Icelandic homes. The Icelandic police turned him over to me without filing a police report. He was returned to the mainland the next day with a note that recommended he be arrested and punished.

BATTLING THOR

THE GEOLOGISTS

The third day of my stay was also the day that the geologists arrived. They pretty much did their own thing, but we occasionally saw them with their thermal suits high on the slopes of the volcano on the windward side. I found that somewhat amazing, considering that there were rocks blowing out of the volcano that were bigger than houses (See figure118).

Figure 118. Geologists on the volcano

One lone geologist explored the rim, as captured by this shot (See figure 119).

Figure 119. Geologist on the upper edge of the volcano

81

EUGENE DALE SCHWARTZLOW

THE *NATIONAL GEOGRAPHIC* PHOTOGRAPHER

On the fourth day I was on Heimaey, a *National Geographic* photographer joined us. We took him under our wing and offered him food and a place to rest. I explained to him that all the military were under strict curfew rules and were not allowed to leave our CP area without my approval. Later that night, the photographer bribed one of the juniors enlisted, and he took him up to the lava flow. He had no protective clothes and didn't seem to care if he was endangering one of my men. When I found out about it, I was not happy and let him know he was no longer welcome. He left and was last seen standing out on a cooled portion of the lava flow shooting into the volcano's "jaws."

His article later appeared in *National Geographic*, and the photos of the military working hard to help the Icelanders were not included or mentioned.

OFFICER TROUBLE

The first shift of volunteers I took to the island consisted entirely of enlisted personnel because I needed workers and not a group of officers standing around in harm's way. The second group of volunteers arrived with a note from the naval station CO. He asked me to allow the two navy lieutenants to work for the navy chief. I reluctantly accepted them. I pulled both aside and discussed the rules. They assured me that they would just roll up their sleeves and do what the chief asked. About halfway through the day, I stopped in to see how they were doing. The chief said they had grabbed their cameras and were down at the lava flow. I grabbed my operations chief and a couple of large Marines, and we found the lieutenants. I checked with Sveinn, and he had an Icelandic fishing boat leaving in an hour. When I saw the lieutenants, I told them what I thought of their disobedience of my orders, and I took them down to the dock. Shortly thereafter, I ordered them to get on the Icelandic boat. Within a few minutes, they gathered up their belongings and were on board the boat. That got them out of my hair for the moment, but I heard much about it in the days that followed. I later learned that an approaching storm forced the boat far out to sea, and the two had spent the entire night sick in quarters aboard the boat.

NO-MAN'S-LAND

Early in the operation, we had drawn lines on the map of homes that were under so much ash that we would not try to save them or their contents. We called it "no-man's-land". On occasion, I drove into that area to look over the town. It was dangerous business because we had to guess where the streets were. If the scoria showed a depression, that was usually a house's roof that had collapsed. Please note the houses are buried, and the vehicle's tire tracks are where we believed the roads were. Here's a picture of no-man's-land (See figure 120).

BATTLING THOR

Figure 120. "No Man's Land"

On one occasion, I stopped and rested my foot on what was left of a streetlight. (See figure 121).

Figure 121. Captain "S" in "No Man's Land"

EUGENE DALE SCHWARTZLOW

THE VOLCANO WALL COLLAPSES
Late during my stay on the island during one of the more active sessions of volcanic activity, the entire wall of the new volcano decided to come to town. Here's how it looked in the morning after the left wall collapsed (See figure 122).

Figure 122. The wall of the volcano collapsed.

It was still very active that morning (See Figure 123).

Figure 122. Activity continued

Magma had got under the wall and moved it toward town. By noon, the entire side of the cone was flat, and the base of the volcano had shifted all the way to town. In fact, the flow stopped right on the line on my map where we had determined we couldn't save the homes that were that close to the volcano.

THE GAS SCARE

Several days after I got to the island, I was joined by a toxicologist, Lieutenant Betts, from America who was there to measure the gases in the sewer system of the island. He joined my staff but was there in support of a request from Sveinn. He spent several days crawling in and out of sewers and taking readings throughout the area. One day, he reported to Sveinn, and I that the sewers were filling with methane gas. He theorized that the red-hot lava would soon reach the methane and that it would set off a chain reaction that would blow up the entire town. When Sveinn told his staff, panic ensued. Nearly everyone wanted off the island. Then calmer heads prevailed, and several of the islanders decided to stick it out. We were given the option to evacuate. I gathered everyone together and gave each person a choice. I told them that I was staying, but they each had to decide if they wanted to be evacuated. I was not putting pressure on them, because it was a big gamble. Fifty percent of my people decided to leave. By evening, the departees were back on the mainland. The rest of us stayed on and worked. In a few days, the lava breached the sewer system, and the methane gas did not ignite. I asked the toxicologist what happened. He again went into the sewers and informed me that another product of the volcano was CO_2 and that it had served as a natural fire extinguisher, which prevented oxidation from taking place. It made it impossible for the gas to explode. I was very pleased with the explanation and the results.

PRAYING TO THE OLD NORSE GODS AND CHRIST

Throughout the eruption, I noticed one interesting fact—the Icelanders spoke of Thor more than they spoke of God. They held nightly candlelight vigils at the village church. They prayed as both Christians and believers of Thor. I must admit, I did some talking to my God as well (See figure 123).

Figure 123. Col S at the village church (a symbol of hope)

The Christian church became one of the most photographed sites on the island. It seemed to stand in defiance of Thor's mighty hammer (See figure 124).

Figure 124. The village church.

FOLLOW-UP ACTIONS

My part in the rescue effort ended on the thirteenth. The work continued. The actions shifted from salvage work to maintenance efforts. Explosive experts were brought in to consider altering the lava flow path. They quickly rejected such ideas.

The dirt wall was pushed up even higher to help protect the town. All the while, the lava mounded higher and higher (See figure 125).

Figure 125. The building lava after the wall collapse

It seemed to work for a while. On 7 March, the sand dredge, Sandy, using a 70 cm pipe, started to pump water onto the flow day and night. These efforts certainly helped the morale of the people, but the volcano continued to follow the path of least resistance.

RENEWED HOPE

Shortly after I returned to the mainland, one of the papers ran a story that showed the pigeons had returned to the island. They said that was a sure sign that the cycle of life continues, and that everything would be okay eventually. It was a prophecy that proved to be very accurate. See figure 126.

EUGENE DALE SCHWARTZLOW

Figure 126. The pigeons return to Heimay.

THE GRAND FINALE

When it was all over, the lava had not destroyed the town, and the harbor was better than ever as seen by this aerial photo. Most of the town had been saved. The Westmann islander's fishing industry had been spared (See figure 127).

BATTLING THOR

Figure 127. Heimay from above after 20 days

RELIEF EFFORTS

Once the initial rescue effort was completed and the phase of the operations called "maintenance" began, the process of healing was initiated. Packets of scoria and postcards were sold to raise money for those who lost everything. It was a great example of man taking care of their fellow man (See figure 128).

Figure 128. Fund raising packets of lava.

AWARDS AND RECOGNITION

Upon the conclusion of American support, the government of Iceland awarded an Icelandic Humanitarian Award to Rear Admiral Behling, Colonel T., Captain McDonald, and several members of the admiral's staff for their contribution. The Icelanders honored none of the volunteers who did the work.

As the commander of the Iceland Defense Force, Rear Admiral Behling sent a thank you message. I received a mimeographed copy. The contents were as follows:

> Subj: LETTER OF APPRECIATION
>
> The members of the Civil Defense Council of Iceland have asked me to convey to you their sincere thanks for the prompt and efficient assistance given by the forces under your command, during the critical rescue period after the start of the volcanic eruption in *Vestmannaeyjar*, January 23 this year. (Para) The unselfish response to our call for help and the high degree of professional skill and devotion to duty shown by every single man in the various and demanding tasks assigned to him was highly achieved. (Para) We do not mention by names but hope you will express our gratitude to everyone concerned. Unquote.
>
> To the above message, I wish to add my personal "well done" to everyone involved in this massive effort. I desire that this message be passed to all hands. RAdm John K. Beling.

PERSONAL RECOGNITION

The Commanding Officer of Marine Barracks was disappointed by the level of recognition shown by his superiors in the chain of command. To express his appreciation for what I had accomplished, he recommended me for a Navy Commendation Medal. It was for my achievements for my entire stay on Iceland from 3 March 1971 to 14 May 1973 but made special mention of the period 2 February to 5 March when I served as the OIC of the Iceland Defense Force Detail.

EUGENE DALE SCHWARTZLOW

FINAL NOTE

My greatest reward for the volcano rescue effort was the experience itself. My adventure in the Land of Frost and Fire was a great one. I will never forget the sights and sounds of land being created. I will never forget the hard work creativity, and dedication of my small band of 100 volunteers who served their fellow man without reward. They were the best kind of ambassadors of goodwill, and they made me proud to be their boss and to be an American.

FOOTNOTE

According to my Icelandic friends, Thor is the Norse God of Thunder. He is a son of Odin and Jord and one of the most powerful gods. He is married to Sif, a fertility goddess. I chose the title *Battling Thor* because of the Icelander's frequent references to Thor, who was constantly causing the earth to roar with each strike of his hammer. The volcano created by Thor is now called *Eldfell*.

ABOUT THE AUTHOR

Eugene Dale Schwartzlow was born in Wisconsin on the fourth month and fourth day of 1944. He is a graduate of the University of Wisconsin–Whitewater with a Bachelor of Business Administration degree. He joined the US Marine Corps on 5 May 1966. He served in the Republic of Vietnam from February 1968 to February 1969 as a first lieutenant. Gene retired from the Marine Corps as a colonel on 30 June 1997 after thirty years, ten months, and nine days of active service. He received the Bronze Star with Combat V while serving in Vietnam.

Some of his other awards include the Defense Superior Service Medal, the Legion of Merit, the Defense Meritorious Service Medal, the Meritorious Service Medal, three Navy Commendations, the National Defense Medal, the Joint Chiefs of Staff identification badge, the Defense Information Systems Agency Europe badge, the Joint Meritorious Service ribbon, the Presidential Unit Citation, the Vietnam Campaign Medal, the Vietnam Service Medal, the Vietnam Cross of Gallantry, and other lesser awards.

Colonel Schwartzlow served as an infantry, logistics, and communications officer.

Gene has kept logbooks all his life and has written over 1,483 short stories about his experiences. He wrote his first book, *Airborne Marine* as a matter of personal therapy and to capture the history of his journey through life for his grandchildren and others that are interested. In particular, he wanted to show the many veterans who suffer from PTSD or other torments a way to release themselves from the burdens of war that they carry. It was published in 2023.

His second book, *30 Years, 10 Months, 9 Days*, was printed in limited quantity in April 2024. It is an overview of all his years of active service. It covers all twenty-two of his duty stations and stories about the significant events that occurred while there. Only thirty copies were printed. Electronic copies are available via sharing on Google Drive.

EUGENE DALE SCHWARTZLOW

His third book, *Battling Thor*, was completed in 2024.

He has completed nineteen other books about his life that he shares on Google Drive. They include an eight-book series entitled *Gullible's Travels* and others, such as *Fish Tales*, *Jagaermann*, *Book of SCUBA*, *Grandpa's Wisdom*, *Contemplations*, *Timelines of a Life*, and *Colonel's Kernels*. Perhaps someday, they too will find their way onto the bookshelf.

He is currently working on another book entitled "Scouting with Mr. S" which covers his 19 years as a scoutmaster/scouter in Virginia, Hawaii, Okinawa, and Switzerland. He hopes to have it published in late 2024.

Gene currently lives with his wife in Edgerton, Wisconsin, and spends his days writing, enjoying the outdoor world and traveling to see his sons, John, and Karl, and his "dear darling daughter" Anne, their spouses and greatest grandchildren in the world—Joshua, Noah, Lia, Sydney and Dylan.